THE
POPCORN
BOOK

Tomie dePaola's

THE POPCORN BOOK

Holiday House  New York

For Florence Nesci, who taught me how to pop the
best popcorn in the whole wide world.

The publisher wishes to thank Martha Small
(Otata'veenova'e) for her expert review of the text.

The Library of Congress has cataloged the prior edition as follows:
DePaola, Thomas Anthony.
The popcorn book.
SUMMARY: Presents a variety of facts about popcorn
and includes two recipes.
1.   Popcorn—Juvenile literature. [1. Popcorn]
I. Title.
TX799.D46   641.6'5'677   77-21456

40th Anniversary Edition
ISBN 978-0-8234-3985-0 (hardcover)
ISBN 978-0-8234-4060-3 (paperback)

YES, THE POPCORN'S IN THE REFRIGERATOR.
MOM, CAN WE MAKE SOME POPCORN?
YUMMY!
TONY
TINY

"Popcorn is the oldest of the three main types of corn. There is field corn, which we feed to animals like cattle and pigs; sweet corn, which is the kind we eat; and popcorn."

"The indigenous peoples of the Americas discovered popcorn thousands of years ago.

"The Aztecs called popcorn *momochitl* and used it for food and decoration. The Lucayan people of present-day San Salvador ate and sold popcorn and used it as jewelry. Before they arrived in the fifteenth century, Spanish colonizers had never seen popcorn before!"

FIRST, I HEAT UP THE PAN.

"But popcorn is even older than that. In a bat cave in New Mexico, archaeologists found some popped corn that was 5,600 years old."

"And 1,000-year-old popcorn kernels were found in Peru. They could still be popped."

NOW, THE COOKING OIL.

"The indigenous peoples of the Americas had many different ways to pop popcorn.

"One way was to put an ear of corn on a stick and hold it over a fire.

"Oiling the cob could keep kernels attached even when they popped. The Ho-Chunk, also known as the Winnebago, were particularly fond of oiled popcorn on the cob."

"Another way was to throw the kernels right into the fire by the handful.

"The popcorn popped out all over the place, so there was a lot of bending and running around to gather it up."

OK. NOW IT'S HOT ENOUGH TO ADD A FEW KERNELS

"The people of the Haudenosaunee, also called the Iroquois Confederacy, popped corn in clay pots.

"They would fill the pots with hot sand, throw in some popcorn, and stir it with a stick.
"When the corn popped, it came to the top of the sand and was easy to get."

"People of many indigenous nations
were fond of popcorn soup."

SOUP?

"The Algonquins introduced popcorn to English colonists.

"The colonists liked it so much that they served popped corn for breakfast with cream poured on it."

NOW, HERE'S THE PART I READ FIRST.

"Popcorn is best stored in a tight jar in the refrigerator, so the kernels keep their moisture.

"If the kernels dry out, there will be too many 'old maids' left at the bottom of the pan. 'Old maids' are unpopped kernels."

IT DOESN'T LOOK LIKE ENOUGH.

"Popcorn only pops because the heart of the kernel is moist and pulpy and surrounded by a hard starch shell.

"When the kernel is heated, the moisture turns to steam and the heart gets bigger until the shell bursts with a 'pop.'"

ARE YOU SURE YOU DIDN'T PUT TOO MUCH POPCORN IN THE PAN?

OF COURSE NOT, SILLY!

"Some people tell the story that inside each kernel of popcorn lives a little man. When his house is heated, he gets so mad that he blows up."

"There are different kinds of popcorn: White hull-less and yellow hull-less are the ones most commonly sold in stores.

"The smallest type is called 'strawberry' because it has red kernels and the ears look like strawberries.

"'Rainbow' has red, white, yellow, and blue kernels. It is sometimes called 'calico.'

"There is black popcorn, too, but all of it pops white.

"The biggest kernels are called 'dynamite' and 'snow puff.'"

SHAKE
SHAKE
SHAKE!

"After popcorn is popped, most people like to put melted butter and salt on it.

"But if salt is put in the pan before the kernels are popped, it makes the popcorn tough."

SHAKE SHAKE SHAKE!

"There are many stories about popcorn. One of the funniest and best-known comes from America's Midwest.

"One summer, it was so hot and dry that all the popcorn in the fields began to pop.

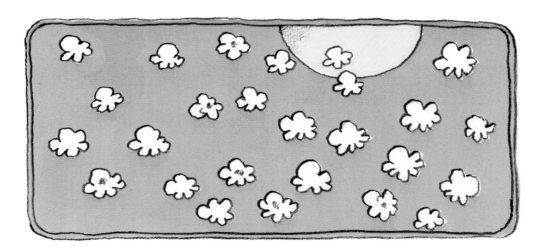

"In no time at all, the sky was filled with flying popcorn."

"It looked so much like a blizzard, everyone put on mittens and scarves and got out the snow shovels."

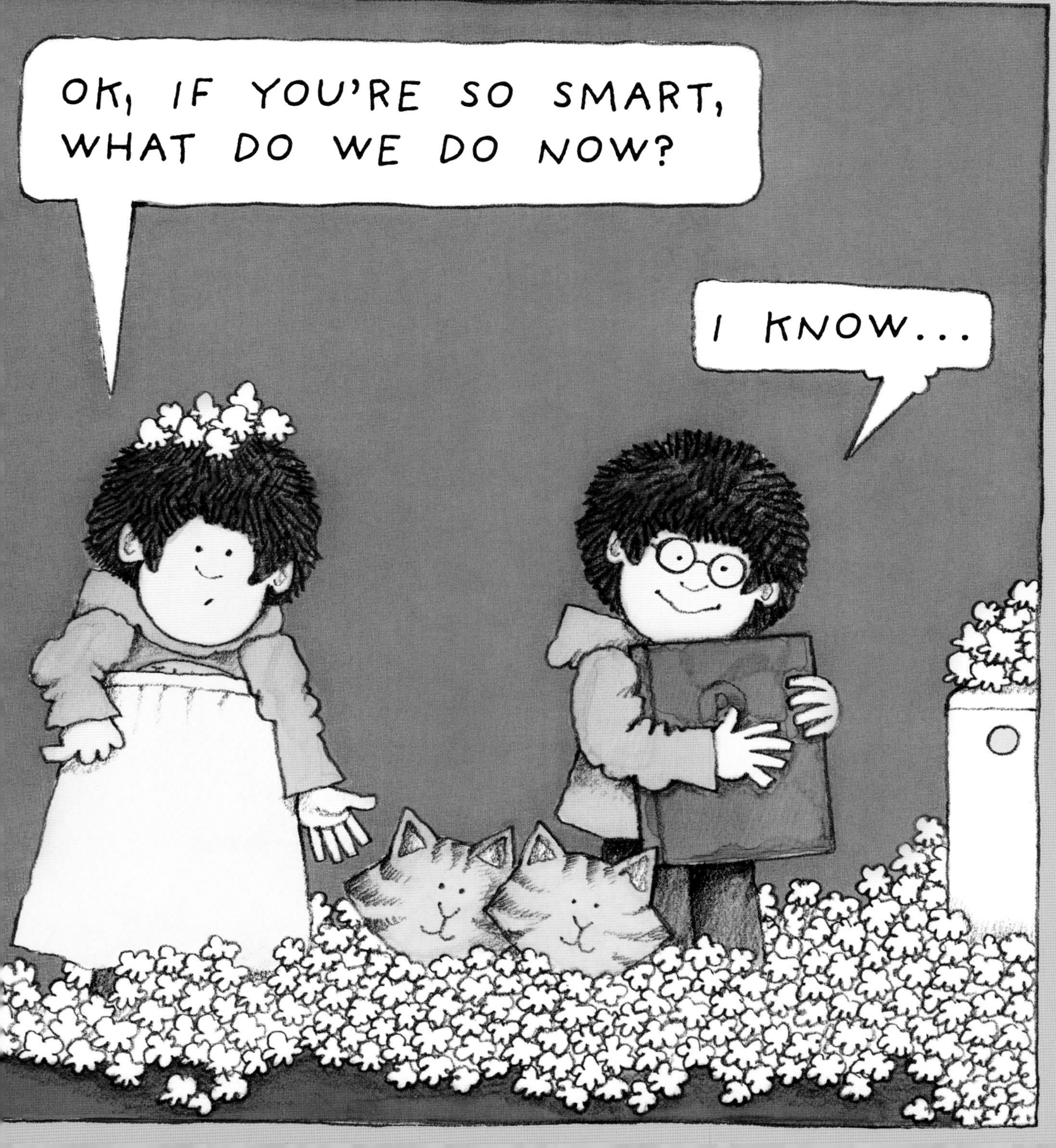
OK, IF YOU'RE SO SMART, WHAT DO WE DO NOW?
I KNOW...